A Time To Heal

Protecting Children & Ministering to Sex Offenders

The Reverend Debra W. Haffner

A LifeQuest Publication

A Time To Heal

Protecting Children & Ministering to Sex Offenders

Rev. Debra W. Haffner

For further information, contact: LifeQuest, 6404 S. Calhoun Street, Fort Wayne, Indiana 46807; DadofTia@aol.com; 260-744-6510.

This book is based on careful research and presents the best practices of which the author is aware. No policy dealing with a convicted sex offender, however, can guarantee that all children, youth, and vulnerable adults in your congregation are safe. Each situation is unique. The author and the publisher are not psychiatrists, law enforcement officers, or attorneys. This book is not a replacement for consultation with relevant authorities regarding situations that arise in your congregation.

ISBN 1-893270-31-9

Library of Congress Control Number: 2005924628

Manufactured in the United States of America
Our thanks to Evangel Press for their help in the production process.

To my brothers and sisters in ministry, who seek to bring about a world where sexuality is celebrated and sexual and relational justice reign.

Table of Contents

Acknowledgments

Many people and congregations participated in the research and development of this manual. I interviewed many ministers and congregational leaders who have faced this difficult issue in their congregations. Because many asked for our conversations to remain confidential, I am including no names here but I am grateful for their honest sharing. I also benefited from the wisdom of several colleagues during conferences I attended throughout the two years that I worked on this manual.

Much of the research for and writing of this manual was conducted under a contract from the Unitarian Universalist Association to develop an online handbook for Unitarian Universalist congregations. The online version can be read at www.uua.org/cde/ethics/balancing/index.html. The UUA graciously gave me permission to adapt this work for churches and synagogues from other denominations. I am grateful for the support of the Reverend Tracy Robinson-Harris and Claudia Hull from the UUA for their support and commitment to this project as well as their willingness to share its results.

A task force met in January 2004 to review an early draft of this manual. Task force representatives included the Rev. Patricia Tummino, the Rev. Dr. William Stayton, Dr. Steve Brown, Dr. Steve Thomas, and Joan Tabachnik. We were joined by the Reverends David Hubner and Pat Hoertdoerfer from the Unitarian Universalist Association for a day of spirited discussion and debate. This manual is better because of their contributions, insights, and expertise.

I am grateful for the wisdom, review, and suggestions provided by Rev. Steve Clapp and Holly Sprunger from Christian Community. I am appreciative beyond words for their support of my ministry and the work of the Religious Institute.

Debra W. Haffner

Foreword

I had only been pastor of the congregation for two months when Dennis asked to speak with me in response to a sermon on forgiveness. He told me that he had done something for which he had never been able to forgive himself and for which he was not certain that God would forgive him. He had molested a nine-year-old girl and a ten-year-old-girl. The incidents had taken place in another state ten years before his conversation with me, and he had served a three-year prison sentencc and an additional two years on parole.

Following his release from parole, Dennis had moved both to escape the relatively small community in which almost everyone knew about his crime and to be closer to his mother who was in failing health. He had ended up as a member of the church I pastored because of his mother's strong involvement in the congregation and because of his own desire to grow closer to God.

His mother and a couple of her close friends knew about his past incarceration and the reasons for it, but no one else did. Filled with self-loathing and a determination not to offend again, Dennis had set his own guidelines to keep himself away from any temptation to repeat his offenses. He would not teach or work with children or youth under any circumstances, in the church or in other community roles. He came across to me and to others as a responsible, friendly, but somewhat shy person. It was not surprising to me that he had been asked to teach children's Sunday school on three different occasions, and I was certainly relieved when he shared with me that he would never accept such an invitation.

At the time he poured out his heart to me, he had been involved in the life of the congregation for almost three years without incident or suspicion. He had decided to trust me with the knowledge of his past both because the burden of keeping it a secret weighed on him so heavily and also because he wanted help in grasping the possibility that God really would forgive him for such sins.

Debra Haffner's excellent book *A Time to Heal* unfortunately did not exist at the time of my conversation with Dennis. The information in this book would have made me less fearful of the possibility that Dennis might reoffend. The guidance to have a team of persons to help deal with such situations would have lifted from me the burden I accepted personally of deciding what to do in response to the information Dennis shared with me. I think the decisions that I made were responsible ones, but I should never have accepted that burden.

A Hospitality Challenge

My work at the level of the local church now is only as a volunteer pastor in my home congregation. My ministry for many years has been one of research, program development, and writing through an organization called Christian Community, whose purpose is improving the health of congregations and the communities in which they minister. Much of that work has been in the area of hospitality. With my Christian Community colleagues, I've authored or edited several resources to help expand the hospitality of faith communities: *Widening the Welcome of Your Church; Hospitality: Life in a Time of Fear; Worship and Hospitality; The First Thirty Seconds: A Guide for Greeters and Ushers;* and *Public Relations Kit: Help from a Hospitality Perspective*.

The discovery of a sexual offender who wants to participate in the congregation or who is already involved in the congregation stands as one of the most difficult hospitality issues that a congregation and its leadership can face. The Hebrew Bible and the New Testament speak strongly about forgiveness, for example:

> Psalm 32 speaks of the joy of forgiveness: "Then I acknowledged my sin to you, and I did not hide my iniquity; I said, 'I will confess my transgressions to the Lord,' and you forgave the guilt of my sin." **Psalm 32:5**
>
> When a woman was charged with adultery, Jesus said to those who thought she should be stoned: "Let anyone among you who is without sin be the first to throw a stone at her." The crowd dispersed, and Jesus said that he did not condemn her. **John 8:1–11**

The reality of forgiveness and the imperative of hospitality must be balanced against the absolute responsibility of the faith community to keep all participants safe. Keeping people safe, however, involves much more than restricting the activity of a known sex offender. As Debra Haffner so accurately says in this book: "The person who is sexually interested in children whom no one knows is a much greater risk to children than the sex offender we do know about."

This excellent book provides the tools that faith communities need to:

- Determine under what circumstances, if any, a convicted sex offender may be involved in the congregation.

- Determine how to respond if someone in the congregation is accused of a sexual offense.

- Be sensitive to and supportive of persons in the congregation who have been victims of abuse.

- Develop and implement strategies that will keep children in the congregation safe and which will prevent sexual abuse from happening.

Who Needs To Read This Book

Debra Haffner shared the concept for this book at a dinner in Indianapolis, Indiana, with Stacey Sellers and me. As I listened to her talk about the complex and difficult issues involved, I realized that this was a very important book, and I feel privileged in having played a role in bringing it into print.

This book certainly will be of interest to both regional judicatory and national denominational executives with responsibilities for clergy and congregational health. Bishops, district executives, district superintendents, presbytery executives, conference ministers, diocesan staff, program staff, and other staff have already dealt with these issues or may be called on to do so in the future. These are persons to whom congregations often turn when needing guidance on such challenges. In our increasingly litigious time, the denominational executives and the denomination itself may be at risk if poor decisions are made. The larger concern, however, is not concern with liability but balancing the need for hospitality and forgiveness with the need to create a safe environment and to be sensitive to victims.

Clergy and leaders in a faith community confronted with a crisis will find this book invaluable. A church or synagogue that has just learned that a sexual offender wants to attend or that a member has been accused of a sexual offense will find Debra Haffner's guidance of immense value. My hope, however, is that this resource will be widely read by clergy and leaders in faith-based institutions which are not going through a crisis at all. A congregation that waits until there is a crisis to consider these issues will be at a significant disadvantage in comparison to one that has taken positive steps to keep children safe and to prepare for any problems that might arise.

I also hope that this resource will be widely read by judges and correctional officials, including probation and parole officers. This book is in no way a legal guide, but it can offer some significant help to persons who are determining how to best help the restoration of offenders to constructive life in the community without endangering others.

In doing the research for this book, Debra Haffner learned that some probation and parole officers actively encourage offenders who are not incarcerated to consider involvement in a faith community. Because those persons so often suffer feelings of isolation, the support of people in a congregation has the potential to improve the lives of these offenders and perhaps to decrease the possibility that they will offend again. This book can help persons making such recommendations do a better job of letting the offender know what to expect and knowing how to relate to the faith community.

I also hope that persons who have been sexual offenders will read this book. It can help them better understand the fears that persons in congregations have about the presence of a sexual offender and can better prepare them for the right kind of approach to a minister or rabbi. In fact a sexual offender wanting to be involved in a congregation might do well to take a copy of this book to an appointment with the minister or rabbi, thus providing a resource and showing sensitivity to the issues involved and the restrictions which are needed.

As I read the pages of the Hebrew Bible and of the New Testament, I do not find restrictions placed on forgiveness or on hospitality. We are not told that there are certain categories of sins that cannot be forgiven or that there are certain categories of people to whom the doors should be closed. I have seen the help of the religious community and the power of God transform the lives of many people.

But I also remember the fear that ran down my spine when Dennis told me what he had done and I realized that he had been involved in the congregation for almost three years without anyone being aware of his background. Because of his own commitment to change, he in fact abided by the kind of limited access agreement that Debra Haffner recommends in this book even though such an agreement was not required since his offender status was not generally known. This book also makes clear that when offenders have the kind of commitment to change that Dennis did, they are not likely to reoffend.

Not every offender, however, has the self-discipline that Dennis did. Keeping children safe in the church involves a proactive approach on the part of our congregations. I commend this book to your careful reading and study with one final caution.

I want to share these important words from the copyright page (which, in my experience, people rarely read): This book is based on careful research and presents the best practices of which the author is aware. No policy dealing with a convicted sex offender, however, can guarantee that all children, youth, and vulnerable adults in your congregation are safe. Each situation is unique. The author and the publisher are not psychiatrists, law enforcement officers, or attorneys. This book is not a replacement for consultation with relevant authorities regarding situations that arise in your congregation. It is also not a substitute for prayer and God's guidance in the decision-making process.

Steve Clapp
President
Christian Community

Introduction

- A person who is a known sex offender is invited by one of the lay leaders of the congregation to join the faith community.

- During a pastoral care session, a man reveals that he feels like he "is on fire around children."

- A 12-year-old (who attends religious education in the congregation) is babysitting a four-year-old boy, who later that evening tells his parents that the babysitter asked him to touch his penis.

- A person who used to be a member of the congregation writes the rabbi (who has never met him) to say that he is about to be released from jail for a sex offense and wants to return to the congregation.

- A convicted sex offender decides that the restricted access agreement he has been asked to sign is too punitive at one congregation and begins to attend another church in the area.

- A newly settled minister of one month discovers that a person in the faith community was arrested for child molestation over 15 years ago; when the previous minister departed, he never told anyone about the offender.

• A long-standing member of the congregation is charged with uploading child pornography to an Internet bulletin board.

These are all situations involving sex offenses—that have happened in faith-based communities around the United States. And in each of these real-life cases, the clergyperson and congregational leaders didn't know what to do. One minister reports that "this was the most difficult decision I have faced in 15 years in ministry." These situations can exacerbate people's most painful personal histories, and congregations often experience divisive conflicts over how to respond.

This manual is designed to help.

Child sexual abuse is a devastating social and public health problem. It is also a crime. One half a million children are thought to be sexually abused each year.[1] These children are violated in the most soul-scarring ways, and in the vast majority of cases, by people they know and trust. And the results are often pernicious and life-long: many survivors of child sexual abuse experience depression, anxiety, post-traumatic stress syndrome, reduced sexual desire, and problems with intimate relationships in adulthood.[2]

---

[1] Stop It Now!, "Child Sexual Abuse: Facts About Abuse and Those Who Might Commit It." MA: Stop It Now!, 1998.
[2] Edward Laumann, et al., *The Social Organization of Sexuality*. IL: University of Chicago Press, 1994, 346.

Note to Survivors of Child Sexual Abuse

Reading this manual or having your congregation decide to include people with a history of sexual offense(s) may exacerbate your feelings of physical, emotional, or spiritual pain. The work described in this manual must be done in conjunction with efforts to address the experiences and needs of survivors and victims as well. If you are a survivor who is still struggling with these issues, please consider talking to your minister or rabbi. Or contact www.rainn.org for an organization or therapist near you.

Many people think that dealing with sex offenders is a new challenge for churches and synagogues, but the fact is that there have always been people who are sexually attracted to children in congregations. In *every* congregation, there are abusers, victims, survivors, and bystanders of childhood sexual abuse. The recent crisis in the U.S. Catholic Church dramatically illustrated that people we love and admire may turn out to be sex offenders, causing irreparable damage to people's lives. Protestant and Jewish faith communities are not immune. Most sexual abuse occurs among family members, and clergypersons and lay leaders may not be aware of the abuse that is currently occurring among families in their congregations.

As a result of a 1996 federal law, every state now has a notification law for sex offenders who have served prison time and are back in the community. The federal law required states to pass laws that convicted sex offenders register with a local law enforcement agency after release and that states make these registries available to the general public. Over time, each state and the District of Columbia adopted statutes modeled after the federal legislation, referred to as Megan's Law, in memory of Megan Kanka, a seven-year-old girl, raped and murdered by a neighbor who, unknown to her family, was a convicted sex offender.[3] In 2000, the Supreme Court found the laws constitutional. These registries include people who have committed a wide range of offenses, from child molestation to rape to exhibitionism and voyeurism to 19-year-olds who had sexual intercourse with their 15-year-old boyfriend or girlfriend and were turned in by irate parents. It is estimated that as many as half a million people may be listed on these registries; the State of California alone has more than 75,000 people listed.[4]

Despite these shockingly high numbers of registered sex offenders, the vast majority (88%) of sex offenses are not reported.[5] The vast majority of people who commit sex offenses do not serve time in prison or receive mandated treatment. The fact is that even with registries, there is no way to know for

---

[3] www.epic.org/privacy/meganslaw.
[4] To find out how to obtain a local registry, contact the local police department or sheriff's office. The KlaasKids Foundation—www.klaaskids.org—has an updated list of state laws based on Megan's Law. Click on "Legislation" to be directed to your state's law and registry.
[5] Joan Tabachnik, personal communication.

sure who may abuse children. And the person who is sexually interested in children whom no one knows is a much greater risk to children than the sex offender we do know about.

Every faith community has an obligation and a commitment to keep children safe—from the person who is known to have a history of molesting children and from those whose sexual attraction to children is unknown to anyone but themselves. There are policies and practices that congregations can adopt to assure that the possibility of sexual abuse is greatly reduced. There are also policies and procedures that will help a congregation offer a worship community to a person with a history of sex offenses.

This manual is based on three premises:

1. Clergypersons and lay leaders have a responsibility to assure that children are safe in congregations from sexual abuse, sexual assault, and harassment *even* or perhaps *especially* when it is not known if there is an offender in the congregation. Indeed, there is a responsibility to assure that congregations are sexually healthy faith communities, free of sexual harassment, abuse, and exploitation for all of our members—children and adults, visitors, and staff.[6]

2. Clergypersons and lay leaders have a responsibility to offer reconciliation and

---

[6] For more information about creating a sexually healthy faith community, see *A Time to Build: Creating Sexually Healthy Faith Communities*. CT: Religious Institute, 2001.

forgiveness to all who sincerely seek them, and to provide a congregational home to all who want one, while honoring that in the case of an individual with a history of sex offenses, there must be limitations on congregational involvement. That commitment means that only in rare cases will a person be denied total access to congregational life. Congregations can provide compassion, forgiveness, affirmation, and protection against opportunities to harm others again.

3. Clergypersons and lay leaders have a responsibility to educate themselves about child sexual abuse and healthy childhood sexuality as well as background on sexual offenders, and only then to develop a process to make good decisions. They must be willing to listen, to use a democratic process, and to be humble about their own certitudes in creating these policies.

This manual is first about primary prevention. We hope that by raising the issues surrounding sexual abuse and sex offenders, congregations can institute policies before there is a crisis. Leaders in congregations may want to think, "these issues don't affect us. After all, no one in our congregation would do these types of terrible things." Unfortunately, even the "nicest people" may do these types of things. One estimate is that between seven and 10% of the population may have a sexual orientation that involves arousal by children. And although many of these people will never act on their feelings, some will. With the advent of sex offender registries, everyone can know when a convicted sex offender enters the faith community.

If the congregation does not address these issues before they occur, there is likely to be a sense of panic and crisis when a sex offender starts attending activities at the congregation, if someone in the congregation is accused of abuse, or when the clergyperson, director of religious education, or another member finds out that a congregation member has a history of abusing children or youth. (If you are in the midst of one of these situations and do not have policies in place, you may want to first go to the boxes immediately following this section on pages 25 to 28, For a Crisis Situation.)

This manual will provide background information on child sexual abuse, sexual abuse prevention, pedophiles, and others who abuse children. There are three myths about sex offenders that must be addressed for a community to deal with this issue without prejudice and unnecessary panic.

MYTH 1: The greatest threats to children are known sex offenders or strangers.

The fact is that in 90% of the cases of child sexual abuse, the abuser is an adult the child knows and trusts: they are parents, stepparents, grandparents, other relatives, babysitters, teachers, coaches, and yes, clergy and religious educators. More than eight in 10 sexual abusers are never reported.

No policy dealing with convicted sex offenders will assure that the children in your congregation are safe. Each faith community must have a commitment to assuring that congregations are safe places for all children, youth, and vulnerable adults. In addition, congregations must be committed to providing compassionate support to those who struggle with a personal history of child sexual abuse or face this problem today in their own families.

MYTH 2: Almost all sex offenders will reoffend.

The research tells us that **the vast majority of treated sex offenders will not reoffend.** The fact is that sex offenders can resume healthy lives in the community, including not committing other offenses, *if* they have completed treatment and *if* they have a commitment to never abuse another child. In a comprehensive review of more than 61 studies, all treated sex offenders had a reoffense rate for another sexual crime of less than 13%.[7] In other words, 87% of sex offenders in these studies who received treatment did *not* commit another offense.

MYTH 3: Sexual abuse happens to other people.

The fact is that a significant minority of adults has survived histories of child sexual abuse. And, child sexual abuse occurs in all types of families, even "nice families," without regard to religion, ethnicity, or economic status.

There are minimum policies that every congregation can consider in order to keep children

---

[7] Howard J. Snyder, "Sexual Assault of Young Children as Reported to Law Enforcement: Victim, Incident, and Offender Characteristics." DC: National Center for Juvenile Justice, 2000, NCJ 182990, 13.

and youth safe and to build the foundation for dealing with a convicted sex offender.

Here's a quick self-assessment. Do you:

1. Have a Sexual Misconduct and Abuse Response Team with primary responsibilities for these issues?

2. Make sure that the clergyperson, the director of religious education, and the board chair know the state laws for reporting concerns about abuse to children? Do all volunteers in the religious education program receive annual training on what to do if they suspect child abuse or child sexual abuse?

3. Have a screening form for all employees, regardless of position, and all volunteers who work with children and youth asking them directly about possible histories of sexual offenses?

4. Have each staff person and each volunteer who works with children and youth sign an agreement to teach form that includes information about sexual abuse and harassment?

5. Have a draft of a Limited Access Agreement or checklist for convicted or accused sex offenders that can be used and adapted if this situation arises?

6. Include education about child sexual abuse prevention in the religious education

program at least twice during elementary school and once during middle school and high school?

7. Hold an annual adult education program on sexual abuse prevention for parents and families?

8. Have two adults present in each class or program for children and youth as well as in cars transporting young people to activities?

9. Have a referral list of community organizations and therapists who specialize in sex abuse prevention and treatment in case they are needed?

10. Have support groups or counseling available to those who have survived child sexual abuse?

A congregation with a serious commitment to child sexual abuse prevention will answer yes to each of these questions. This manual will address how to implement these policies.

For a Crisis Situation

This manual is designed as primary prevention, but perhaps you are reading it because there is a crisis facing your congregation. A person who has served time for a sex offense against children has come to the minister or rabbi and said they want to become part of the congregation. A member of the staff has scanned the sex offender registry and has noticed that a congregation member's name is on it. A long-standing member of the congregation who is a teacher has been accused by a student of sexual misconduct. A 12-year-old in the congregation is found fondling a three-year-old while he is baby-sitting. And so on.

Almost uniformly, congregations that have dealt with convicted sex offenders report that there has been some degree of panic among members when the facts become known. Indeed, in some cases, congregations have become seriously divided over the issue of whether a sex offender should be allowed to attend worship services. In some cases, the clergyperson has refused participation. In many cases, those most alarmed about the possibility of a sex offender attending worship are themselves survivors of childhood sexual abuse or assault. This past history continues to affect people in their adult lives, and this kind of situation can evoke past trauma and an unwillingness to address even the possibility that a person with a history of sex offenses can safely attend.

Here are steps to follow:

1. Do not panic. There is no question that this will be a difficult issue for the clergyperson, the religious educator, the board, and the members of the congregation who find out about it. This is why clergy are trained to be a Non-Anxious Presence. This issue is likely to take several months if not longer to be resolved well.

2. Ask for help. Contact your denomination's office that deals with sexual abuse or family issues. Contact Christian Community about arranging for a consultant who can help you. Contact a treatment provider in the community who has expertise in these issues. Read through this manual.

3. Understand that this is likely to be a difficult and divisive issue. Some parents of children may threaten to leave the congregation if the offender is allowed to attend worship at all. Some people who were themselves sexually abused as children may be especially affected as old hurts are reopened. Provide opportunities for all sides to be heard. Recognize that reasonable people may disagree. Allow time for and facilitate the opportunity for people to share their feelings *before* you begin to develop policies and guidelines.

4. Form a committee to develop a plan. The minister or rabbi or the chair of the board should not deal with this situation alone. If you don't already have a "Response Team" (see page 43), form a small committee consisting of the clergy, the director of the religious education program, a key member of the leadership of the board, and if possible, two or three congregational members who have expertise dealing with people with a history of sex offenses or sex abuse prevention.

Develop a plan together.

5. Seek outside expertise. It is unrealistic to expect that the members of a church board of trustees have the skills to evaluate an individual situation or assess safety issues in a particular context. It is reasonable for the members of the Response Team, including the clergyperson, to meet with the person and ask for written permission to contact their therapist and parole officer. In the case of someone who has completed mandated treatment, ask the person to meet with a trained therapist (who is a member of ATSA: Association for the Treatment of Sexual Abusers) for an evaluation of his or her risk potential.

6. Be sure pastoral care is available to those who are survivors of abuse. It can't be said enough; some people who are survivors of sexual abuse or assault may need special attention at this time. Make sure the pastoral care providers have time to see people and that referrals are available.

7. Remember that the accused person also deserves support. There is likely to be a feeling of revulsion or antipathy towards this person, and the immediate response may be to want to isolate that person completely. The congregation can recognize and support with compassion even as it addresses the clearly inappropriate and perhaps criminal behavior. It is also important to reach out to that person's spouse and/or children.

8. Educate, educate, educate. If the whole faith community knows about this situation, it may make sense to call for a congregational meeting. An education session with outside experts on child sexual abuse and sex offender treatment can be very helpful. In some cases, it may be helpful to ask the offender to tell their story to the board or to a congregational meeting. As a part of the educational process, consider the teachings of Scripture on forgiveness, protection, and hospitality. Keep the community as a whole informed as the leadership of the congregation works to develop or implement the policies.

9. Seek legal counsel and counsel from your insurance company. Know what the state and local laws are. Be sure you are protecting the congregation from lawsuits. Check with your denomination on your liability.

10. Allow enough time. The process for developing an informed, just response to this situation will likely be time-consuming, messy, emotional, and not satisfying to all parties concerned. Recognizing that this will take time, may not be perfect, and is always difficult will help heal some of the issues that are being raised.

11. Pray for all involved. Pray on a daily basis for the offender, for past victims of the offender, for people in the congregation who may have been victims in the past, for the family of the offender, and for the congregation as a whole.

Information on Child Sexual Abuse, Pedophilia, and Sex Offenders

Before a congregation begins to develop policies and procedures on sexual abuse prevention and responding to a sex offender, it must first educate itself about child sexual abuse and sex offenses. Childhood sexual abuse is a pervasive and devastating social problem. It is important to know the facts about child sexual abuse, pedophilia, and sex offenders. The information in this section will provide the reader with a rudimentary understanding; readers are encouraged to contact the organizations listed on pages 88 to 91 for more information, as well as to read the cited resources themselves.

Definitions

Child sexual abuse is any

> "sexual act imposed upon a child who lacks emotional, maturational, and cognitive development. Authority and power enable the perpetrator, implicitly or directly, to coerce the child into sexual compliance. The ability to lure a child into a sexual relationship is based upon the all-powerful and dominant position of the adult or older adolescent perpetrator,

> which is in sharp contrast to the child's age, dependency, and subordinate position."[8]

The abuse can be intrafamilial—between a child and a family member or person in the role of a family member, or extrafamilial—between a child and someone outside the family. Incest is a specific term for sexual contact between persons who are prohibited to marry by virtue of their familial relationship.

Sexually abusive behaviors range from nudity, disrobing, exhibitionism, to oral, anal, or vaginal sex. Child sexual abuse can include:

- Touching a child's breasts, genitals, and anus.
- Having any type of intercourse with a child.
- Encouraging a child to watch or hear adult sexual acts.
- Using an object, instrument, or body part to penetrate a child's genitals or anus.
- Having a child touch another's genitals.
- Using a child in erotica.
- Showing erotic or pornographic materials to a child.
- Photographing a child in sexual poses.

Sexual abuse of children is common. According to a number of studies, between 17 and 25% of women report that they were sexually abused before the age of 18, and between 10 and 15% of men

[8] Claudia Crawford, Child Sexual Abuse Evaluation, Treatment, and Legal Issues, Handouts prepared for workshop for American Association of Sex Educators, Counselors, and Therapists, September 2003.

were sexually abused before the age of 18. In a national study of adults aged 18 to 59, about 12% of the men and about 17% of the women reported that they had been sexually touched as children.[9] Both boys and girls are sexually abused, but abuses against girls predominate. Eighty-two percent of all juvenile sex crime victims under the age of 18 are female.[10] Experience with childhood sexual abuse does not vary by ethnicity, race, social status, or education background of the parents.[11] Most children do not tell anyone the abuse has taken place. In a study of adults who remembered being touched sexually as a child, only one quarter of the women and one in six of the men remembered that they had told someone about this sexual contact with an older person.[12]

Portrait of the Abuser

The myth is that children are sexually abused by strangers or known sex offenders. The reality is that strangers account for a small proportion of the abuse. Children know their abusers well in 90% of the cases—they are parents, family members, neighbors, clergy, coaches, and teachers.[13] Family friends and relatives are the primary offenders; family friends are more likely to offend with boys and relatives to offend with girls. One in seven girls is abused by a father, stepfather, or mother's boyfriend,

---

[9] Laumann, et al., 340.
[10] Snyder, 4.
[11] Ibid.
[12] Laumann, et al., 42.
[13] Stop It Now!, "Child Sexual Abuse: Facts About Abuse and Those Who Might Commit It."

although only three percent of boys are abused by people in these categories.[14] One quarter of offenders of victims ages 12 through 17 are family members.[15] Nearly five out of every six sexual assaults of juveniles occurred in someone's home, not a public place.[16]

Men are much more likely to be sexual offenders than women. Ninety-six percent of all offenders in sexual assaults of all ages reported to law enforcement agencies are male.[17] Girls are primarily sexually abused by men, while the boys are abused more often by women but also by men. The younger the child, the more likely the offender is female: six percent of the offenders who sexually assaulted juveniles under the age of 18 were female, but 12% of the offenders with victims under six were female.[18]

The risk to girls is greatest from adult men (63%), followed by adolescent males (28%). The risk to boys is greatest from adolescent women (45%), followed by adolescent men (25%) and then older men (38%).[19] It surprises people to learn that 70% of abuse to boys is by teenagers; few congregations have policies that address the possibility that adolescent babysitters may inappropriately touch children.

Children may also commit sex offenses. Children and adolescents are the offenders in 40% of

---

[14] Laumann, et al., 342.
[15] Snyder, 10.
[16] Snyder, 13.
[17] Snyder, 17.
[18] Ibid.
[19] Laumann, et al., 342.

the sexual assaults of victims under the age of 12.[20] Forty percent of the offenders of children under the age of six were other juveniles under the age of 18.[21] Sixteen percent of juvenile offenders were under the age of 12.[22]

Pedophilia

Pedophilia and pedophiles are terms that are often used incorrectly to describe someone who has had sexual contact with children. This information is presented to increase knowledge of pedophilia and clarify the use of terminology.

Clinical pedophilia is not the same as child sexual abuse or offending; a person can be diagnosed as having clinical pedophilia without committing criminal sexual acts with children. Many pedophiles may not be child sex offenders—they are attracted to children but do not act on those feelings. Many people who sexually molest children are not pedophiles; these are people who are primarily sexually attracted to adults, but in a specific situation, molest a child.

The Diagnostic and Statistical Manual of Mental Disorders, or DSM-IV-TR, defines a person with pedophilia as a person who:

> "A. Over a period of at least 6 months, [has] recurrent, intense sexual arousing fantasies, sexual urges, or behaviors

---

[20] Snyder, 13.
[21] Snyder 11.
[22] Snyder, 8.

involving sexual activity with a prepubescent child or children (generally 13 years or younger);

B. The person has acted on these urges, or the sexual urges or fantasies cause marked distress or interpersonal difficulty;

C. The person is at least age 16 years and at least 5 years older than the child or children in Criterion A."

The DSM-IV-TR notes that this definition does not include an individual in late adolescence involved in an ongoing sexual relationship with a 13-year-old. It also asks clinicians to differentiate based on the sex of the preferred child, whether the behavior is limited to incest (a family member), and whether the attraction is exclusive (attracted only to children) or nonexclusive.[23]

Ephebophilia is a preferential sexual attraction to adolescents. It is not considered pedophilia, and given the proliferation of images of sexualized adolescents in the media, it is fairly common. Ephebophilia's legality is determined by state sexual consent laws; in other words, once a young person reaches the state's legal age of consent, it is not a crime to have sex with them. Nepiophilia is a sexual attraction to infants.

Pedophilic behavior usually begins during adolescence or early adulthood. Pedophiles are said to "groom" children. It is rare for their contact to be

---

[23] American Psychiatric Association, *Diagnostic and Statistical Manual of Mental Disorders, Fourth Edition, Text Revision*. Washington, DC: American Psychiatric Association, 2000, 571–572.

forced upon a child. Rather, "they may begin with flattery and gifts or take the child on 'dates' (outings), while proceeding from intimate conversation to sexual talk and sexual touch, gradually getting the child accustomed to each new step." Children who are lonely, depressed, or angry with their parents are most vulnerable to these special attentions.[24]

Treatment and Recidivism

As noted above, most sex crimes against children are never reported, and most sex offenders do not come to the attention of law enforcement authorities. Eighty-four percent of sexual abusers are never reported, and the National Crime Victimization Survey found that two-thirds of sexual assaults against persons 12 and older are not reported to law enforcement.[25]

Nevertheless, since congregations need to know how to respond to people who have been convicted of sex offenses, this information is offered to clarify many of the misunderstandings around treatment and recidivism.

Although state laws and practices vary, in many states convicted sex offenders who are serving time in prisons are not granted parole until they have successfully completed a sex offender treatment program. Once granted parole, states generally require the person, as a condition of their parole, to

---

[24] Harvard Mental Health Letter, "Pedophilia," January 2004.
[25] Center for Sex Offender Management, "Recidivism of Sex Offenders," CSOM Documents, May 2001, www.csom.org/pubs/recidsexof.pdf.

participate for a length of time in a treatment program for sex offenders. State laws do vary, and congregations will want to find out what treatment is available in their county jails and state prisons as well as parole requirements for treatment. A growing number of persons are being charged at the Federal level for offenses related to pornography and child solicitation over the Internet.

Treatment for sex offenders typically includes:

> "[a] cognitive behavioral approach, which emphasizes changing patterns of thinking related to sexual offending and changing deviant patterns of arousal; ...a psycho-educational approach, which stresses increasing the offender's concept of the victim and recognition of responsibility for their offense; and the pharmacological approach, which is based upon the use of medication to reduce arousal."[26]

According to the Harvard Mental Health letter, anti-androgen medications are "the only reliable way, proven in controlled studies, to suppress pedophiliac urges."[27] (Anti-androgen medications reduce the level of testosterone in a user's system, resulting in reduced sex drive.)

There is a generally held perception that sex offenders are untreatable. Indeed, when I conducted interviews with congregations about their experience with this issue, I heard repeatedly that the majority of

---

[26] Ibid.
[27] Harvard Mental Health Letter, "Pedophilia," January 2004.

sex offenders would reoffend. And in several cases, congregations voted to completely exclude the offender from the faith community based on this incorrect assumption. One church that dealt with these issues wrote to their membership, "the social worker explained that while studies in the literature vary substantially on the issue of recidivism rates, she was inclined to accept that repeat offenses were rather likely."

But that isn't true. The review of the literature for this monograph actually shows that **with treatment, the majority of sex offenders will not recommit a sexual offense**.[28] Even with the offenders who are pedophiles, treatment can help change behavior even if it does not change sexual attraction patterns. In a 1998 evaluation of 61 research studies on sexual offender recidivism (known as a meta-analysis) sexual offense recidivism was very low (13.4% of more than 23,000 offenders). The sexual offense recidivism of child molesters was slightly lower—12.7% for 9,603 abusers.[29] In another study, one in five of the extrafamilial child molesters

---

[28] It is important in reviewing research on sex offender recidivism to separate child molesters from other sex offenders such as rapists and exhibitionists, as well as subsequent sexual offenses from all possible criminal offenses committed. Note that in some studies sexual and nonsexual reoffenses are grouped together, leading to much higher reoffense rates. For this manual, only sexual reoffenses are considered. It is also important to recognize that studies are limited because they are only based on reported offenses, not those that might go unreported.

[29] R. Karl Hanson and Monique T. Bussiere, "Protecting Relapse: A Meta-Analysis of Sexual Offender Recidivism Studies," *Journal of Consulting and Clinical Psychology*, 66:2 (1998) 348–362.

recidivated.[30] The Bureau of Justice Statistics of the U.S. Department of Justice reports that only 5.3% of sex offenders were rearrested for a sexual crime within three years of release.[31] Other criminals have much higher rates of recidivism, for example, 38% of those convicted of a violent crime had another offense, as did one third of those with a property offense. In other words, in each of these studies, the majority of child molesters are *never* reconvicted for a sexual offense. It is also important to note that many of these studies include all sex offenders, not just child molesters or pedophiles, and that they are based on reported cases. According to the Harvard Mental Health Letter, "arrests and confessions don't necessarily indicate the true numbers of repeat offenders."[32]

Treatment makes a difference. According to Stop It Now!, "there is a credible body of evidence that suggests that with specialized treatment, some sex offenders can take responsibility for their own behaviors, learn how to identify and control their triggers, and go on to lead healthy, safe, abuse-free lives."[33] In a 2000 study in Kentucky, fewer than one in five (17.6%) of treated non-family offenders committed another sexual offense. But, untreated offenders commit more than twice as many sexual

---

[30] R. Karl Hanson, "Age and Sexual Recidivism: A Comparison of Rapists and Child Molesters," www.psecp-sppcc.gc.ca/publications/corrections/age200101_e.asp.
[31] Bureau of Justice statistics, "Recidivism of Sex Offenders Released from Prison in 1994," www.ojp.usdoj.gov/bjs/abstract/rsorp94.htm.
[32] Harvard Mental Health Letter.
[33] Personal communication, Amanda Horowitz, Stop It Now!, December 2002.

offenses as those who have had treatment.[34] According to the above-referenced meta-analysis of 61 studies, offenders who fail to complete treatment are at higher risk for reoffending than those who complete treatment.[35] In one study of child molesters in treatment, 18% of those receiving cognitive behavioral treatment recidivated compared to 43% who did not participate in a program.[36] This means that it is critical that the decision-makers find out the treatment history of a person who wants to attend the congregation, and speak to the treatment provider about whether the person is likely to reoffend. The person with a history of sex offenses must have accepted his or her responsibility for the offense, understand the gravity of the situation, and be committed to not offending again.

There are also other factors besides completing treatment that are believed to reduce the risk of reoffending. These include

> "realizing the enormity of what they have done, admitting their responsibility, and the harm their sexual violence has caused; support from family and friends on release; establishment of a social network; avoidance of situations involving contact with children; and par-

[34] Claudia Crawford, Child Sexual Abuse Evaluation, Treatment, and Legal Issues.
[35] Hanson & Bussiere, 348–362.
[36] Center for Sex Offender Management, "Recidivism of Sex Offenders."

> ticipation in ongoing treatment and agreement to monitoring."[37]

There are people with a history of sex offense(s) who have demonstrated that they are able to control their impulses, avoid triggers, and thus eliminate any subsequent sexual behavior with children.

Further, **involvement with a faith community may actually lessen the chance that a person will commit another sex offense.** To quote the Methodist Church of the United Kingdom, "for many sex offenders, social isolation and a failure to integrate into an adult community contribute to an emotional lovelessness and poor self esteem that serve to increase the risk of reoffending."[38] To offer sex offenders (who are in treatment or have completed treatment) appropriate support and involvement in a congregation may reduce isolation and increase accountability.

And indeed, turning a sex offender away from a congregation may actually put more children at risk. Rather than letting congregational leadership know that they would like to attend and taking steps to assure their participation is monitored, such persons may decide that the next time, they simply won't share their history and just "hope for the best." The next congregation's children may be put at risk because of your congregation's decision to exclude someone.

---

[37] Methodist Church Reports, "The Church and Sex Offenders," www.methodist.org.uk/status/news/papers/church_and_sex_offenders.htm.
[38] Ibid.

An excellent review article, which is accessible to nonprofessionals, is “Recidivism of Sex Offenders” by the Federal Center for Sex Offender Management. It can be read at www.csom.org/pubs/recidsexof.pdf. An excellent fact sheet entitled “Myths and Facts About Sex Offenders” is also available from the CSOM at http://www.csom.org/pubs/mythsfacts.html.

Congregation Practices

Introduction

A congregation needs to consider three components to assure that theirs is a safe space for children, youth, and vulnerable adults. These three components are:

A. Policies and procedures for educating the adults, youth, and children in the congregation about child sexual abuse and prevention.

B. Policies and procedures for keeping all children safe from sexual abuse.

C. Policies and procedures for responding to a person who has been convicted or accused of sexual offenses against children.

These components will vary by congregation. The size of the congregation, the physical layout of the congregation, the personal histories of the clergyperson and the congregational members, and other factors will influence the implementation of these suggestions. Congregations are encouraged to adapt or modify these suggestions to meet the specific needs of their communities. Guidelines and forms are offered as a template for discussion and deliberation; there is no "one size fits all" approach to these complex issues. Further, this is a process: it may take a year or two to put all of these policies and practices into place. The following recommendations are offered as a starting point of procedures to consider, based on best practices of existing congregational policies and expert advice and consultation.

Ideally, the congregation will have a Task Force on a Sexually Healthy Congregation, which will provide recommendations to the board and the clergyperson on all areas of sexuality: worship, pastoral care, lifespan education, welcoming and affirming congregations, social action, and safe policies. Other congregations may view these needs as distinct and separate. In that case a "Safe Congregations Committee" may be the best place to assign the responsibility of developing these policies and procedures. In other cases, a new committee may need to be formed to deal with child sexual abuse prevention and safety.

However named, this committee will meet to review this manual and its suggested policies. They can review the background information on child sexual abuse prevention and sex offenders and seek assistance from local community resources, their denomination, or Christian Community, Inc. (see the Resources section).

The committee will want to recommend to the board policies to be adapted, amended, or adopted for the screening of all employees and volunteers who come into contact with children and youth and a draft of a Limited Access Agreement or checklist.

The committee, with the advice and consent of the board, will name a Sexual Misconduct and Abuse Response Team generally made up of the clergyperson, a religious education leader, and three members of the congregation, with experience in sexual abuse issues when possible. Gender balance should be given consideration in appointments. Some congregations have developed a panel of six to eight members of the congregation who can be called upon as needed to form a response team. Although some congregations form such a response team only after there has been an allegation, this is unlikely to provide the wisdom and continuity that are helpful.

The Sexual Misconduct and Abuse Response Team will generally have the following responsibilities:

1. Be knowledgeable about community resources for child abuse, treatment for sex offenders, and support groups for survivors.

2. Be knowledgeable about state laws regarding reporting.

3. Be a resource for people to share their concerns.

4. Evaluate applications for religious education teachers and youth group leaders that are flagged by the clergy or religious education professionals in the congregation as needing more information or follow-up.

5. Facilitate annual training for religious education staff and volunteers on issues, policies, and procedures relevant to sexual/physical abuse.

6. Meet with sex offenders to develop a Limited Access Agreement for participation in church activities.

7. Receive allegations of possible abuse, and develop a process for expedient handling of such allegations.

This committee could offer a report at the annual meeting of the congregation. Policies might also appear annually in the congregation newsletter and be included in new member packets.

Component A
Educating Adults in the Congregation

Primary Prevention

It is important that adults in the congregation are educated about the problem of child sexual abuse and how to prevent it. There are a number of ways that everyone in the community can become involved in sexual abuse prevention. This can include educating people about the prevalence of child sexual abuse, programs for parents on educating their children about healthy sexuality including sexual abuse prevention; and making sure that staff, lay leaders, and volunteers know how to handle a suspected case of child abuse or child sexual abuse. The congregation's policies on these issues should be included in new member packets and reviewed periodically with the congregation.

Primary prevention is key. Possibilities for ways to share information include:

- Sermon on child sexual abuse
- Bulletin or order of service insert on policy

- Healing service for survivors
- Clergyperson's letter to members
- Newsletter articles
- Adult religious education class
- Sex abuse prevention component of sexuality education programs
- Open congregational meeting
- Annual training for religious education teachers, board, and staff
- Outside speakers
- Relationships with local organizations and experts to consult with should the need arise

Programs for parents on talking with their children about sexuality, including how to keep their children safe from abuse, can be offered in the congregation, and are especially important if they are not offered elsewhere in the general community. Parents need support in providing their children with healthy messages about sexuality that are age appropriate. They also need to be able to recognize the signs of possible child sexual abuse. They need to know that while sex play between children of similar ages is often healthy curiosity, sex play between children who are more than three years apart is most often problematic. They need to know that it is expected for children to play doctor or "you show me yours, I'll show you mine," but that any type of penetration, whether with fingers, objects, or penises, is not typical childhood behavior but a sign to be concerned. Parents need to know that it is important to screen child care workers and babysitters for histories of sex offenses and to ask that day care and nursery school caregivers, coaches, scout leaders, after school workers, etc. be screened by the sponsoring agency.

Possible Signs of Childhood Sexual Abuse

- A child with an unusual discharge from the penis or vagina
- A child who compulsively masturbates in public, after being told repeatedly that this is private behavior
- A child who tries to get other children or adults to touch his or her genitals
- A child who is more interested in sex play than playing with friends, going to school or other activities
- A child who manually stimulates or has oral or genital contact with pets
- A child who repeatedly draws pictures with the genitals as a primary focus
- A child who engages in sex play with a child more than three years apart in age
- A child who engages in penetrative behaviors during sex play

All of these behaviors could also arise from other causes. Tell the minister or rabbi about your concerns. If you see these behaviors in your own child, stay calm but do make an appointment as soon as possible with your child's pediatrician or a mental health professional who specializes in child sexual abuse and assessment.

(Adapted from Debra W. Haffner, *From Diapers to Dating: A Parent's Guide to Raising Sexually Healthy Children,* Second Edition. New York: Newmarket Press, 2004, used with permission.)

When Abuse is Suspected

Adults in the community also need to know what to do in cases where they suspect abuse. According to Stop It Now!,

> "We adults have to learn to see when people are acting strange around our kids. And we have to learn what to do when we think a person is harming a child in a sexual way. It's a lot like what you do when you see someone who is drinking and planning to drive: you try to get them help so they don't hurt someone. There are warning signs that can help us figure out whether someone we know might be interested in children... the most important piece of information we can use to protect our kids is knowing who to call for advice, for help, or to report a case of abuse."[39]

Stop It Now! has a confidential toll-free hotline for assistance on what to do if you are concerned about potential abuse but are unsure how to proceed: 1–888–PREVENT. Stop It Now! hotline staff will walk you through the options that are available and what might be done to get help for everyone involved.

[39] Stop It Now!, "Child Sexual Abuse: Facts," 2.

Possible Signs of an Adult Being an Abuser

Do you know an adult or older child who:

- Refuses to let a child set any of his or her own limits?
- Insists on hugging, touching, kissing, tickling, wrestling with or holding a child even when the child does not want this affection?
- Is overly interested in the sexuality of a particular child or teen (e.g., talks repeatedly about the child's developing body or interferes with normal teen dating)?
- Manages to get time alone or insists on time alone with a child with no interruptions?
- Spends most of his or her spare time with children and has little interest in spending time with someone his or her own age?
- Regularly offers to babysit many different children for free or takes children on overnight outings alone?
- Buys children expensive gifts or gives them money for no apparent reason?
- Frequently walks in on children/teens in the bathroom?

If you answered "yes" to some of these questions, talk to that person. If you are uncomfortable, but don't see these signs, be sure to trust your instincts and ask questions. For information and advice on how to talk to someone, please call the Stop It Now! toll-free Helpline at 1–888–PREVENT. Reprinted with permission.

Laws in each state vary on reporting suspected child sexual abuse. The minister or rabbi, the director of religious education, and the chairperson of the board need to thoroughly understand the law on reporting, but it is important that that every person who works with or comes in contact with children in the congregation knows what is required if he or she suspects abuse. Stay aware of updated state legislation. At least annually, there should be information in the congregational newsletter about what a member should do if they suspect abuse.

The National Child Abuse Hotline (by telephone at 1–800–4–A–Child or their website http://childhelpusa.org) provides state-by-state information on how to report abuse in each community. In every state, doctors, nurses, dentists, mental health professionals, social workers, teachers, day care workers, and law enforcement personnel are required to report suspected abuse. In some states, clergy are mandated reporters. In about 20 states, any person who suspects abuse, regardless of professional background, is required to report it.[40] The law generally requires that adults are to report anything that would be suspicious of abuse or neglect by a reasonable person.

Regardless of who is specified by the law to be a mandated reporter, any teacher or youth group leader who suspects abuse should immediately contact the rabbi or minister, who will proceed to implement the required actions. If a teacher or youth group leader has reason to suspect that a child would be endangered by returning home, and they cannot

[40] American Psychological Association, "Protecting Our Children From Abuse and Neglect," www.apa.org/pi/pii/abuse.html.

reach the clergyperson or the director of religious education, the adult should contact the police or Child Protective Services immediately, and then leave an emergency message for the clergyperson. In general, Child Protective Services will ask the child's name, date of birth, parent's name, details of the suspected abuse, the name and residence of the offender and their relationship to the child, and, if possible, the address where the abuse occurred.

It is important to remind oneself that it is not the function of the congregation—not the clergyperson, the director of religious education, the chair of the board or any member—to conduct an investigation into a case of alleged abuse. If a child tells you a story, listen carefully and affirm their courage for telling you. Do not ask investigative questions, which can hurt prosecution at a later time. Tell the child that you will contact the minister or the rabbi and that you will help them get help. And then be sure to follow up.

Support for Survivors of Sexual Abuse

There are likely to be people in the congregation who themselves were abused sexually as children. According to national statistics, as many as one quarter of adult women and one in seven adult men experienced at least one incident of inappropriate sexual touching as a child. And for a significant minority this has had life-long ramifications. In every congregation, there are people of all ages who have abused, people who have committed abuse against others, and people who have remained silent when they knew abuse was going on. We need to offer ministry to all of these people.

Congregations can offer support groups for survivors of childhood sexual abuse. There can be healing services for survivors. The clergyperson and other pastoral care providers can obtain special training in providing counseling to people who have been abused. It is important to have referrals for people who need more intense therapy for past sexual abuse issues (see the list of resources on page 90). A referral agreement/relationship with the domestic violence and sexual assault programs in the area is also critical.

Component B
Keeping All Children Safe

Basic Congregation Practices

Although the primary purpose of this manual is to help congregations deal with a known sex offender, the reality is that that alone does not keep children safe. The fact is, to put it bluntly, the sex offender who is known and who has been through treatment is not the person who is most likely to sexually abuse children in the congregation. **The person who isn't known, but who has children's trust, poses the greatest threat to children.**

Adults who work with children and teenagers in congregations have a special responsibility to help keep children safe. One denomination's handbook said it this way:

> "...Whether acting as a youth advisor, chaperone, childcare worker, teacher, minister, ...or in any role, adults have a special opportunity to interact with young people in ways that are affirming and inspiring to young people and adults....
>
> While it is important that adults be capable of meaningful friendships with the young people with whom they work, adults must exercise good judgment and mature wisdom in using their influence with children and young adults and refrain from using young people to fulfill their own needs. Young people are in a

vulnerable position when dealing with adults and may find it difficult to speak out about inappropriate behavior by adults....

[A]dult religious leaders need to be people who: ...have a social network outside of their religious education responsibility in which to meet their own needs for friendship, affirmation, and self esteem [and] are willing and able to seek assistance from colleagues and religious professionals when they become aware of a situation that requires expert help or intervention."[41]

There are basic policies that should be considered by every congregation. They are:

1. No person who has been convicted of any act of sexual misconduct of any kind shall be permitted to be involved in any religious education for children and youth, children's worship, event for children, or youth group activities.

2. Any incident or disclosure of sexual abuse of a child by either a staff member of the church or a volunteer at the church working with children should be reported as required by state law.

3. There should be a minimum at all times of two adults present in each classroom, at

---

[41] Unitarian Universalist Association, *Congregational Handbook*, 1995.

youth group meetings, and other events involving children and youth in the church. The staff religious educator or lay chair of the religious education committee will circulate among classrooms, partially to assure that this policy is in effect. If a teacher or leader calls in absent, the other teacher or leader will ask a parent or another adult to stay in the room during the class. Classes will generally not take place with only one adult present. In some small congregations, this policy may not be realistic, but the widespread practice of this protects both children and adults.

4. Every person seeking paid employment at the congregation, regardless of the position, and every volunteer who will come in contact with children, will complete a Screening Form. (A sample screening form is on page 79.) Every employee and every volunteer who comes in contact with children will receive a copy of the Safe Congregation's policies. No person will be allowed to work with children if they answer yes to any question about sexual misconduct.

   If something in the Screening Form raises suspicion, there will be a criminal background check as well as a check for the name on the sex offenders' registry. The local police department can provide information for your state on how to conduct a background check.

The Screening Form in and of itself may help deter a pedophile from further attempts to volunteer or work at the congregation. Most pedophiles will look for places with easy access to children; this type of screening form indicates that your congregation is not such a place.

5. Every employee and every volunteer who works with children will annually sign an Agreement To Teach Form that addresses ethical issues. A sample of such a form is on page 83.

6. All persons volunteering to work with children and youth will ordinarily have been associated with the congregation for at least six months to one year. Exceptions should be made only by the rabbi or minister upon recommendation of the clergy at another congregation where the volunteer has provided such services.

7. Every person, whether employee or volunteer, who works or comes in contact with children, will attend training on child sexual abuse prevention and reporting requirements. This training will include:

   - Definition of child abuse
   - Sexual and physical abuse symptoms
   - Basics of child sexual development and expected behaviors by age
   - What constitutes inappropriate touch and behaviors
   - Congregation's Safe Policies and ethics policy

- Rationale behind screening procedures
- Reporting procedures for observed or suspected child abuse and child sexual abuse

The preteens and teenagers who babysit during congregation events will also be screened. Ideally, babysitters will have Red Cross or similar babysitting training. As with adults, teens and preteens should only babysit in pairs or even larger groups. Information about sexual abuse should be part of their annual training, including the damage that inappropriate sexual touching could do to a child and the consequences that exist if someone is found touching a child. These potential babysitters also need to be told that if they feel tempted to touch a child sexually, they need to tell a grownup about these feelings and receive help. This kind of attention in the preservice training may help screen out young people who might sexually act out or propel them to get help. If the congregation has a comprehensive sexuality education program, preteens and teens can receive this information as part of that program.

9. Positive relationships should develop between adult advisors and teens in youth groups and classes. Adult youth leaders, however, need sufficient maturity to recognize appropriate and inappropriate ways of relating to teens. Sometimes a mentoring relationship will develop between a youth and an adult, and some churches develop formal mentoring programs to

encourage such relationships. Unfortunately, an unhealthy relationship initiated by a sex offender may masquerade as such a relationship. Therefore, such relationships need to be entered into carefully and steps must be taken to assure that they are beyond reproach. Any relationship between an adult leader and a youth in their care outside of congregation activities should be completely transparent. Parents must know about the relationship and give explicit consent to time together. The clergyperson or director of religious education should also be informed. This will keep not only the youth safe, but assure that the adult is protected from false accusations.

Educating Children and Youth for Prevention

A high quality sexuality education program taught at the faith community is one of the best safeguards for sexual abuse prevention. Children who learn that their bodies are good, that their sexuality is a gift from God, how to make good decisions, and the language to communicate accurately and effectively about sexuality are also being prepared to respond when faced with abusive behaviors, to assert their right to control their own bodies, and to tell an adult if such behaviors occur. For a list of faith-based sexuality education curricula, visit www.religiousinstitute.org/curricula.html. Also, for information on youth and sexuality resources, visit Christian Community's website at www.churchstuff.com.

Churches and synagogues can assure that all children develop the skills to recognize when an adult is acting in an inappropriate manner towards them as well as a sense of what to do if an adult tries to engage them in inappropriate behavior. They must know the names of the parts of their body, and they must trust that adults will believe them if they "tell on" an adult. It is good practice to at least offer a sexual abuse prevention lesson in the congregation, once during early elementary school (K–2), once during later elementary school (3–5), and once during middle school. A program for high school students on date rape prevention and sexual harassment is also advisable. Christian Community's book *The Gift of Sexuality: Empowerment for Young People* can help youth avoid dangerous situations and also help them learn positive assertiveness.

Children who understand that their bodies belong to them and that no one else should touch any part of them without their consent and permission are less likely to be vulnerable to an adult. Every child, from the age of three onward, can learn "No, Go, Tell"—say no to the abuse, leave the situation immediately or as soon as possible, and tell a parent or caregiver if someone tries to hurt them or asks them to keep a secret about touching. Age-appropriate messages for a preschooler include:

- Your body belongs to you.
- Other children's bodies belong to them. You should not touch another child's body in any way without their permission.
- Tell your parent if any other person makes you feel bad or funny or does something that makes you think, "uh-oh."

- You can tell someone, even a grownup and even a relative, not to touch your body if you don't want to be touched.
- If someone touches you and tells you to keep it a secret, tell a parent or another grownup anyway.

Age-appropriate messages for an early elementary schooler include:

- No adult should touch a child's genitals except at a doctor's office.
- Sexual abuse occurs when an older, stronger, or more powerful person looks at or touches a child's genitals for no legitimate reason.
- A person who is sexually abusing a child may tell the child to keep the behavior secret.
- Tell a parent right away if unwanted or uncomfortable touching occurs.
- Most adults would never abuse children.
- Both boys and girls can be sexually abused.[42]

---

[42] These are adapted from the SIECUS Guidelines for Comprehensive Sexuality Education and my book for parents, *From Diapers To Dating: A Parent's Guide to Raising Sexually Healthy Children*, Second Edition. New York: Newmarket Press, 2004.

Component C
Guidelines for Involving Sex Offenders

Introduction

The third key component of a commitment to keep children, youth, and vulnerable adults safe in our congregations is developing a policy and a set of procedures to use when a person who is a known pedophile or a sex offender wants to be part of the congregation or an existing member is accused of a sexual offense. It is best to think through these policies and procedures in advance of facing a crisis. (If you are in a crisis situation, you may want to turn directly to page 25 now.) Just because this situation has not yet occurred in your congregation does not mean that you shouldn't be thinking about it. Given the prevalence of child sexual abuse, it is especially important to try to be prepared in advance.

According to the Federal Center for Sex Offender Management,

> "the criminal justice system manages most convicted sex offenders with some combination of incarceration, community supervision, and specialized treatment... the majority are released at some point on probation or parole (either following sentencing or after a period of incarceration in prison or jail.) About 60% of offenders managed by the U.S. correctional system are under some form

of conditional supervision in the community."[43]

And many of them want to attend worship and participate in the life of a faith community. In fact, attendance and membership in a local congregation may be encouraged by their treatment provider and parole supervisor, often to cut down on their social isolation.

There are those who believe that a convicted sex offender never belongs in a faith community. This manual takes another view, based on a review of the literature on sex offenders, interviews with congregations that have successfully integrated a convicted sex offender within adult worship and education, and a theological commitment to forgiveness, restoration, and redemption, even for those who have committed morally repugnant acts. We are committed to helping people atone for their sinful behavior and to make amends to those who have been wronged. The Jewish word "teshuvah" expresses the principle of repentance. When sins are committed against people, the person must admit their wrongdoing, ask the person to forgive them, and then be reconciled by changing the behavior. The Christian faith teaches that all men and women are affected by sin, and stand in need of forgiveness, restoration, reconciliation, and salvation. There are many stories in the Hebrew Bible and the New Testament where people are restored to wholeness. Salvation is offered not just in relationship to God but to community.

---

[43] Center for Sex Offender Management, "Recidivism of Sex Offenders."

As religious communities, we can provide compassion, support, and reconciliation to those who truly have indicated that they have changed and have taken responsibility for their actions. We believe in the healing power of involvement in a spiritual home, and in forgiveness and reconciliation. We must remember that sex offenders who have completed prison sentences and mandated treatment as well as registered with the state have, according to the court system, complied with their punishments. We need to remind ourselves that **the peer-reviewed literature clearly demonstrates that the majority of treated sex offenders do not reoffend.** As faith-based communities, we can provide support and compassion with awareness and vigilance so that all are safe as those who have sexually offended return to or join our church community.

In many ways, the person with a history of sex offenses has the same needs for a faith community as the rest of us: in the words of the United Kingdom Methodist Church, "acceptance, love, a place to worship and join in fellowship, comrades for the journey...." But the sex offender needs to assure that his or her involvement doesn't pose risk to the congregation and also needs protection against false allegations and suspicions.

> "Such involvement needs to include helping him manage his behavior and not get into situations which in the past led to offences.... [A]n offender who truly wishes to participate in the life of the church, who realize the extent of his crime and the difficulty his presence may cause to survivors, and who is truly committed to a new life will understand

> and accept the need for the imposition of restrictions...."[44]

We must assure that convicted sex offenders do not have the opportunity in our congregations to reoffend again and that they avoid situations where they can be accused falsely. The fact is that a person with a history of sex offense(s) against children should **never** be allowed to be with children, work with children and youth, or socialize with children at the congregation. **No person who has been convicted of—or accused of until all charges have been dismissed of—any sexual misconduct can be permitted to be involved in any religious education or youth group activities**.

The core response of the congregation to a convicted or accused sex offender is a *Limited Access Agreement*. A Limited Access Agreement invites the person with a history of sex offenses to participate in adult worship services, coffee hour, committee meetings, adult education, all-adult social events, and well-supervised intergenerational events. It asks the person to avoid all contact with children on congregation property or at congregation-sponsored events. This includes avoiding talking with children and not volunteering or chaperoning children's events, including children's religious education classes, talks with children during worship, and children's activities during intergenerational events. It generally requires the person to remain in the presence of an adult who knows his or her situation at all times when children are present, including, in some cases, asking the person to suggest a group of people to act as companions at church events where

---

[44] Methodist Church Reports, "The Church and Sex Offenders."

children may be present. It denies the person access to keys to the building and asks them to avoid being in the building unsupervised when activities involving children are in session, such as nursery school or youth group. A sample Limited Access Agreement that can be modified based on the feedback of the committee and the individual circumstances of the offender is on page 85. It includes two introductory paragraphs: one for a person who has been accused of a sexual offense, the other for someone who has been convicted. **The overall message to a treated or accused sex offender should be that they are welcome to participate in adult worship, adult social, and adult education activities AND that they must covenant with the congregation to avoid all contact with children.**

There are generally a few ways that the presence of a convicted sex offender becomes known in a congregation. In an ideal world, a person with this background would come to the minister or rabbi before attending the congregation to discuss limits on their participation. Sex offender treatment specialists and parole or probation officers often encourage their clients to do just that. In some cases, people do reveal their backgrounds to the clergyperson. In other circumstances, a congregational member may discover that another member may have a history of sexual offenses. Congregation members should know that in these cases they should make their concern known to the clergy. In other cases, someone may see a familiar name on the sex offender registry. Or, perhaps it becomes known that a long-standing member of the congregation has been accused of a sexual offense.

Steps To Take

1. No matter how the situation is revealed, the minister or rabbi should meet privately with the individual to discuss the concerns that have been raised as soon as possible. The clergyperson may want to check the local sex offender registry before meeting with the person. (If the clergyperson is the one being accused, this manual and these steps do not apply. Instead, the board chairperson and the denomination's office of ministry should be contacted regarding next steps.) If the person is a member of the congregation and has a partner who also attends, then the rabbi or minister should reach out to the partner as well.

2. If the minister or rabbi determines that there is a genuine reason to be concerned, the person should then be asked to meet with the hopefully preexisting Sexual Misconduct and Abuse Response Team (referred to in the following pages as the Response Team). See pages 43 to 45 for more background on that Team. If such a team does not exist, the clergyperson in consultation with the board chairperson should convene such a group, consisting of the clergy, the person responsible for religious education, and if possible at least three members of the congregation who have professional expertise in this issue.

3. The individual should be asked to sign a release so that the clergyperson can contact his or her sex offender treatment provider and current therapist. Ask if those people are members of ATSA, the Association for the Treatment of Sexual Abusers. The therapist and the parole officer should be asked for their professional assessment of the likelihood

that the sex offender will reoffend and whether additional restrictions beyond the standard Limited Access Agreement need to be placed on the person's participation. If the person has been in the community for some time and has previously completed mandated treatment, the committee would be wise to ask the person to go for a professional assessment with a therapist who specializes in working with sex offenders. The congregation may need to provide the funding for this assessment. If the offender refuses permission to contact the therapist or refuses to go for an assessment, the congregation would be right to refuse participation in any congregational activity. (See the box on page 73 for a list of reasons that are appropriate for excluding an abuser from all congregational participation.)

It is beyond the scope and experience of congregations to assess the risk or probability that a sex offender will reoffend. According to the Center for Sex Offender Management, even therapists with special training in treating sex offenders can be wrong. They write,

> "There are no absolutes or magic bullets in identifying these risk factors. Rather, this process is an exercise in isolating factors that are associated with specific behaviors. While this association reflects likelihood, it does not say that all individuals who possess certain characteristics will behave in a certain manner. Some offenders will inevitably commit subsequent sex offenses...

> likewise not all sex offenders who have reoffense characteristics will recidivate."[45]

4. If the assessment indicates that the person has completed or is participating successfully in treatment and is not at high risk for recidivism, the next step is to develop a Limited Access Agreement. If the professional assessment indicates that the person is at high risk for reoffending, it is appropriate to deny that persons involvement in the faith community until treatment is successful at reducing the risk. The Methodist Church of the United Kingdom recommends that

> "a small group should be set up, consisting of approximately five persons, including the minister, persons who have agreed to offer pastoral support for the offender, and accompany them in worship and other church activities, someone with expertise or experience in this field, and someone to represent the wider church community. The group should acquaint itself with any therapeutic program the offender has undergone or will continue to be part of. The group should meet the offender, their probation officer, and other appropriate people so that clear boundaries can be established for the protection of children and youth and to reduce the likelihood of false allegations or suspicions. This group will, at best, operate alongside

[45] Center for Sex Offender Management, "Recidivism of Sex Offenders."

> other agencies in a multi-agency approach to the offender's rehabilitation."[46]

Meeting with the other support people in the offender's life—his or her family, therapist, probation officer—can powerfully demonstrate the faith community's desire to support the person and hold them accountable. If the person has a partner in the community, that person should have input into the Limited Access Agreement as well and be aware of its provisions.

It is important to point out that a person with a commitment to avoiding future abuses will welcome the opportunity for controls on their behaviors. Stop It Now! writes,

> "You can show your support of the abuser's willingness to live a different life that keeps children safe. Your support and watchfulness can help in his or her recovery. It is also a chance to let the abuser know that you are aware of the past and are watching his or her actions today."[47]

All persons with past histories of sexual offenses should be asked to sign a Limited Access Agreement upon entry into the congregation and depending on the circumstances, the person may be asked to re-sign one annually. If the offender refuses to do so, it is then appropriate to deny the person access to congregation functions and church property. An offender who refuses to sign a Limited

---

[46] Methodist Church Reports, "The Church and Sex Offenders."

[47] Stop It Now!, "Child Sexual Abuse: Facts," 10.

Access Agreement should know that if they enter the congregation or its property, they will be asked to leave by a member of the Response Team or the board. If the person further refuses, the local police will be called for assistance.

5. The Response Team should meet at least quarterly with any individual with whom it has a Limited Access Agreement to review the arrangement and address any concerns. If the clergy or the person responsible for religious education changes, as well as the chair of the board, it is important that the departing person inform the new person of this situation to ensure provision of pastoral support for the offender as well as continuity of awareness of the situation.

6. Obtain legal assistance. You may want to contact an attorney about local and state laws. You may also wish to talk with your insurance company about negligence and liability standards.

7. Decide who needs to know. One of the very important and difficult questions is who needs to know that a congregational member has a history of sex offense. Clearly, key people, including the minister or rabbi, the director of religious education, the chair of the board, and the Response Team need to know that the person is attending church, that he or she has agreed not to have contact with children, that he or she has signed a Limited Access Agreement, and that he or she should never be alone with children and adolescents.

Some congregations have chosen to tell the entire congregation that a person with a history of sex offenses has joined the church, and that there is a Limited Access Agreement in place. In some cases, the identity of the person is withheld to protect his or her privacy. In other cases, the person's name is given. According to the Methodist Church of the United Kingdom,

> "there is much to be said for explaining the circumstances to the whole congregation, to promote understanding and support for the individual but also to ensure that church members do not unwittingly allow children contact with the individual concerned. However, this needs to be weighed against any need for confidentiality or pastoral sensitivity... the need to know must be balanced with the danger that the offender may be hounded out of the community (to his detriment and to the greater danger of the other children if he decides to maintain a low profile next time around)."[48]

In the words of one of the reviewers of this document who has worked extensively with sex offenders and argues against the entire congregation knowing the person by name, "it is important to understand that offenders who have served their time and been released into society have rights and can sue a congregation that is unfair, punitive, or not respectful of their rights to privacy regarding information that is given out without their permission." One congregation has devised a policy in between: the congregation knows the policies that have been developed to keep all children safe. The name of a

---

[48] Methodist Church Reports, "The Church and Sex Offenders."

particular person with a history of sexual offending is known to the minister and the director of religious education, and the minister will share that name with any parent who requests it in a private meeting. The board in grappling with the issue of sex offenders in the congregation will want to make the decision about how confidentiality will be handled, and it is that decision that should be communicated to the entire congregation.

A special word concerning small congregations: In many small congregations, it will be inevitable that everyone who is regular in attendance will end up knowing about the presence of a sexual offender or of someone who has been accused of a sexual offense. In those situations, it's far better to have an official meeting with the whole congregation than to let word-of-mouth carry the information. When the congregation meets as a whole, everyone can receive accurate information and have an opportunity to ask questions of the Response Team.

The especially close bonds that exist in some small congregations may make them ideal settings for a convicted sex offender to experience hospitality and belonging without having to lead a secret life. There are some small congregations around the United States that have a predominantly elderly membership and no children actively involved. Some of those faith communities are in a position to offer a safe place to a sexual offender. These are not ministries for every congregation, but faith communities should not too quickly rule out the possibility that they are called to this kind of caring and restoration.

Reasons for Excluding a Person from All Congregational Activities

- Refusal of permission for the rabbi or minister to contact the treatment provider and parole officer.
- Refusal to go for a risk assessment with a qualified therapist.
- Recommendation by a treatment provider that the individual is at too high a risk for recidivism.
- Refusal to sign a Limited Access Agreement.
- Refusal to comply with the requirements of the Limited Access Agreement.

If an individual decides that he or she can comply with these conditions, at that point the process would begin again to reassess the individual and see if he or she could be re-welcomed into the life of the congregation.

Youth Who May Be Abusers

One of the most difficult possible situations is when a teenager or child in the congregation has been accused of inappropriately sexually touching another child in the congregation. The difficulty is that in some cases these children may simply be acting on their sexual feelings impulsively, not quite understanding the importance of boundaries, whereas in other cases, youth and children who engage in sexual activity with younger children may become future adult offenders. If an older child forces sex on a younger child or exposes his or her genitals to a younger child, both of these children will need professional help. If an older child demonstrates inappropriate sexual interest in younger children that doesn't extend to these behaviors, there may or may not be cause for congregational involvement. However, "any child who engages in sex play with a much younger child, or children who coerce or force someone to engage in sex, is beyond normal sexual exploration. If a child is being used in any way to meet the sexual needs of another, then it is sexual abuse."[49] And some children who behave this way are acting out their own history of sexual abuse.

After such an incident comes to the attention of the clergyperson or other staff member, the rabbi or minister should initiate contact individually with the parents of both children to discuss the allegation and

[49] Stop It Now!, "Do Children Sexually Abuse Other Children?" MA: Stop It Now!, 1999, 4.

next steps. In some congregations that I spoke to where this had happened, the clergypersons reported that the parents had simply stopped coming to the congregation rather than seeking help for their children and support from the faith community during what is surely a difficult time.

The minister or rabbi should encourage the parents of the child who was touched to seek an evaluation for this child. Some children may seem unfazed by the incident. However, a child who has been sexually abused, according to Stop It Now!, "needs specialized help and attention to heal from this abuse" through treatment with a specialist, "otherwise he or she might be at risk for further abuse or for showing abusing behaviors." However, with treatment and support, the risk of either further abuse or for abusing is dramatically decreased. The Association for the Treatment of Sexual Abusers (ATSA) or the Safer Society Foundation would be good places to contact for referrals if you don't have a local list of therapists with expertise in this area.

The parents of the child who initiated the sexual contact need to be engaged more thoroughly in discussions about next steps. Depending on state law and the nature of the incident, Child Protective Services may need to be called. Regardless, before that child is allowed to continue to attend religious education, this child should receive an extensive assessment by a child psychologist or psychiatrist with experience with children with sexual behavior problems. It is *not* the responsibility of the rabbi or minister or the Response Team to decide if abuse has occurred, but rather to assure that such an assessment does take place.

While this review is occurring, it is important that the child's religious education teacher be informed of the allegation and for the parents to agree to closely monitor their child before and after the religious education program. It may make sense to remove the child from religious education during this time. It would certainly be prudent for the child not to be allowed unsupervised time with other children until the assessment is complete.

The clergyperson will need to decide if the situation warrants the involvement of the entire Response Team and if so, at what point. If the evaluation finds that this was simply a case of inappropriate boundaries or impulsive behavior, and with the recommendation of the therapist that the child can safely attend church functions with other children, the rabbi or the minister and the parents can meet with the child to discuss the importance of never repeating the behavior, the harm it can do to other children, and the consequences should such a situation occur again.

On the other hand, if the treatment provider reports that the child has a sexual behavior problem that is likely to be repetitive, the clergyperson, the director of religious education, the Response Team, and the parents need to meet to decide how and if the child can safely be involved with the religious education or youth group program. A modified Limited Access Agreement should be developed and signed by both the child and the parents. In some cases, it may be necessary to deny the young person continued involvement with other children until treatment is completed and to consider alternative ways to provide religious education, such as through individual sessions with a religious educator or home schooling.

In some situations, a family will want to bring a teen who has been treated for sexual offenses back into the congregation after treatment is completed. In such cases, the steps for involving an adult offender can be followed, including a Limited Access Agreement signed by both the youth and his or her parents.

In any of these cases, pastoral care and support for the families involved is crucial. This will be very difficult for the parents involved, and they will need the support of their church community, especially the minister or rabbi and the director of religious education. Hospitality and support to these persons are important congregational ministries.

Forms for Congregations

Beginning on the next page are a Model Screening Form For Religious Educators And Youth Group Staff And Volunteers; a Model Agreement To Teach Form; and a Model Limited Access Agreement. These forms may be reproduced for use in congregations or by regional judicatories.

MODEL SCREENING FORM FOR RELIGIOUS EDUCATORS AND YOUTH GROUP STAFF AND VOLUNTEERS

Thank you for your interest in working with the children and youth of our congregation. Our congregation takes seriously the responsibility of assuring the safety of our youth. Please fill out this form and give it to the director of religious education. Thank you for your support in providing a safe and secure environment for all of the congregation's children and youth.

Name

____

First Middle Last

Have you ever used a different name? ___No ___Yes

If yes, please list with dates:

How long have you been attending this congregation?

____

Address

____

Street

____

Town State Zip

Number of years at current address: ___

If you have not lived at this address for at least five years, please list any other addresses over the last five years with dates.

What states have you lived in since you were 18 years old?

Home Phone ____________________

Work Phone ____________________

Number of years at current employment: ____

May we call your current employer for a character reference?
____ Yes ____ No

If not, please tell us why.

A. Have you ever been convicted of any criminal offense?

If yes, please explain.

B. Have you ever been accused of any crimes against a person, including rape, incest, sexual exploitation of a minor, sexual or physical assault of a minor?

If yes, please provide details:

C. Have you ever resigned from employment or been disciplined or terminated by any employer for reasons related to sexual misconduct or child abuse?

If yes, please provide details:

D. Have you ever been convicted of any crimes against a person, including rape, incest, sexual exploitation of a minor, sexual or physical assault of a minor?

If yes, please provide details:

E. Other than the above, is there any fact or circumstance involving you or your background that would call into question your being entrusted with the supervision, guidance, and care of children and youth?

If yes, please provide details:

Congregation History and Prior Work With Children and Youth

List congregations you have attended during the past five years.

Name of congregation	City, State	Dates

List all previous work involving children and youth (list name, type of work performed, person you were responsible to).

Please list two references who are not relatives who have known you for at least three years and who are familiar with your character as it pertains to your experience with children or youth:

1) Name ____________________

Phone ____________________

Address ______________________________________

Relationship to you: ______________________

2) Name ____________________

Phone ____________________

Address ______________________________________

Relationship to you: ______________________

I authorize the congregation to contact references and other congregations to obtain information about my background regarding my character and fitness for work with children and youth. I authorize references to provide such information about me. I hereby release and hold harmless from liability any person or organization that provides information. I also agree to hold harmless this congregation, its trustees, employees, and volunteers.

Further, I understand that a member of the staff may check the sex offender registry and/or contact the local police for more information about my background.

This information will be available only to those responsible for screening staff and volunteers or participating in a response team, or as required by law.

I attest that the above information is true and correct.

____

Signature Date

MODEL AGREEMENT TO TEACH FORM

Adults and older youth who teach children in our faith community play a key role in fostering spiritual development and wholeness. It is, therefore, especially important that those in leadership positions be well qualified to provide the special nurture, care, and support that will enable children and youth to develop a positive sense of self and wholeness. The relationship between young people and their leaders must be one of mutual respect and regard, with the adult leader assuring the safety and well-being of the children in their care.

I have read and understand our congregation's policies on keeping children safe.

I understand my responsibilities to report any concerns I may have about a child in my care who may be suffering from any type of abuse.

I understand children, youth, and adults suffer damaging effects when leaders become sexually involved with young persons in their care. I will not engage in any sexual, seductive, or erotic behavior or any behavior that might constitute sexual harassment, including verbal, emotional, or physical harassment or abuse with any child or adolescent entrusted to my care.

I affirm that I have never been accused of, convicted of, or pled guilty to any sexual crime. I also have not pled guilty to a lesser charge after having been charged with a sexual crime. I have never engaged in any form of child abuse, including sexual abuse. I have never been determined to have engaged in any sexual offenses in any civil, administrative, or ecclesiastical forum or other forum.

If there are any facts or circumstances in my background that call into question my being entrusted with the supervision, guidance, and care of children, youth, or vulnerable adults, I have met to review this information confidentially with our clergy and the person in charge of religious education.

Further, I agree to notify both of them immediately should I be accused of sexual abuse, sexual offenses, sexual harassment, or other sexual improprieties in any venue during the time that I am working with children and youth in this congregation.

____

Signature Date

MODEL LIMITED ACCESS AGREEMENT
CONFIDENTIAL

[Introductory Paragraph in cases of allegation:] A serious complaint or allegation has been made about you to the Sexual Misconduct and Abuse Response Team. That complaint is now under review. While this complaint is being investigated, in order to protect the children and youth in our programs from potential risk, and in order to protect you from further suspicion, we ask you to abide by this interim agreement. Signing this document in no way constitutes a presumption or confession of guilt. This is a routine safety precaution, activated without prejudice toward particular individuals or circumstances. This document will be made known only to the clergyperson, the director of religious education, and the members of the Sexual Misconduct and Abuse Response Team. It will be kept in a locked file in the office.

[Introductory Paragraph in cases of convicted sex offender:] The [Name of Congregation] affirms the dignity and worth of all persons. We are committed to being a religious community open to those who are in need of worshipping with us, especially in times of serious personal troubles. However, based on your background, we have concerns about your contact with children and youth in our congregation. The following guidelines are designed to reduce the risk to both you and them of an incident or accusation. We welcome you to our congregation and our membership, but your participation will be limited in ways to ensure the safety of our children and to assure that you will not be subject to future accusations.

Within these guidelines, the congregation welcomes your participation in adult worship services, coffee hour, committee meetings, adult education, all adult social events, and well-supervised intergenerational events. You are to avoid all contact with children on congregation property or at congregation-sponsored events. This includes the following:

- Please do not talk with children.
- Please do not volunteer or chaperone children's and adolescents' events, including children's religious education classes, talks with children or adolescents during worship, youth group, children's and adolescents' activities during

intergenerational events, and driving children and young people to activities.

- Please remain in the presence of an adult who knows your situation at all times when children are present.

- If a child in the congregation approaches you, either at church or in a community place, politely and immediately excuse yourself from the situation.

- Please avoid being in the building unsupervised when activities involving children are in session, such as nursery school or youth group.

I accept that the following people [Insert names or positions] will be told of my circumstances in order for them to protect the children/young people for whom they care.

I have reviewed this covenant and agree to abide by its provisions. I agree that if I violate this agreement, I will be denied access to future church functions and church property.

I understand that this contract will be reviewed every ___ months and will remain for an indefinite period.

____
Signature Date

____

____
Witness Date

____
Clergyperson Date

____
Religious Educator (if applicable) Date

____
Board Chair Date

Conclusion

The issues addressed in this manual are complex and difficult. They cause us to seriously examine our commitment to forgiveness, reconciliation, and redemption. They require us to think about how we are to honor our commitments to providing a safe place for all to worship, learn, and socialize. They ask us to address issues of sexuality, both the celebration of God's gift to us and the exploitation of this sacred gift, with intention and integrity. We can keep our children and youth safe from sexual abuse *and* we can offer ministry and a congregational home to people who have been treated successfully for sexual offenses. We are called to do no less.

Resources

Stop It Now! has developed a more comprehensive list of organizations that deal with sexual abuse; visit www.stopitnow.org.

General Information about Child Sexual Abuse

FaithTrust Institute (formerly known as Center for the Prevention of Sexual and Domestic Violence)
936 N. 34th Street, Suite 200
Seattle, WA 98103
206–634–1903
www.faithtrustinstitute.org

ChildHelp USA—National Child Abuse Hotline
1–800–4–A–CHILD
Hotline is staffed 24 hours, 7 days a week.
National Clearinghouse on Child Abuse and Neglect Information
U.S. Department of Health and Human Services
330 C Street SW
Washington, DC 20447
800–394–3366
http://nccanch.acf.hhs.gov

Prevent Child Abuse America
Formerly National Committee to Prevent Child Abuse
200 S. Michigan Avenue, 17th Floor
Chicago, IL 60604
312–663–3520
www.preventchildabuse.org

Stop It Now!
P.O. Box 495
Haydenville, MA 01039
1–888–PREVENT
www.stopitnow.org
(Their comprehensive resource guide includes a more extensive list of resources than are presented here.)

Information about Sex Offenders

Center for Sex Offender Management
8403 Colesville Road
Suite 720
Silver Spring, MD 20910
301–589–9383
www.csom.org

National Adolescent Perpetration Network
Kempe Children's Center
1825 Marion Street
Denver, CO 80218
303–864–5300
www.kempecenter.org

The Safer Society Foundation, Inc.
P.O. Box 340
Brandon, VT 05773
802–247–3132
www.safersociety.org
(also treatment referrals)

For Referral to a Treatment Provider for an Assessment

Association for the Treatment of Sexual Abusers (ATSA)
4900 S.W. Griffith Drive, Suite 274
Beaverton, OR 97005
503–643–1023
www.atsa.com

The Society for the Advancement of Sexual Health
P.O. Box 725544
Atlanta, GA 31139
770–541–9912
www.ncsac.org

See also The Safer Society Foundation and the National Adolescent Perpetrators Network as well.

Support for Congregation Members and Constituents

Parents Anonymous
675 W. Foothill Blvd.
Suite 220
Claremont, CA 91711
909–621–6184
www.parentsanonymous.com

Sexual Assault Recovery Anonymous
P.O. Box 16
Surrey, BC, V3T 424
Canada
604–874–2616
866–466–7272

Survivors of Incest Anonymous
P.O. Box 190
Benson, MD 21018–9998
410–893–3322
www.siawso.org

Voices in Action
8041 Hosbrook Road, Suite 236
Cincinnati, OH 45236
1–800–7–Voice–8
www.voices-action.org
(support for victims of incest and child sexual abuse)

For Insurance Issues

Church Mutual Insurance Company
3000 Schuster Lane
P.O. Box 357
Merrill, WI 54452
800–554–2642
www.churchmutual.com

Sexuality Education & Consultation

Christian Community
6404 S. Calhoun Street
Fort Wayne, IN 46807
800–774–3360
www.churchstuff.com

Religious Institute on Sexual Morality, Justice and Healing
304 Main Avenue, #335
Norwalk, CT 06851
www.religiousinstitute.org

Here's valuable information from another LifeQuest/Christian Community publication:

FAITH MATTERS: TEENAGERS, SEXUALITY, AND RELIGION
By Steve Clapp, Kristen Leverton Helbert, and Angela Zizak
EXECUTIVE SUMMARY

How do religious faith and congregational involvement influence the sexual values and behaviors of teenagers?
Faith Matters shares what the authors learned in a study of 5,819 teenagers involved in faith-based institutions. *Faith Matters* surveyed teens from Protestant, Roman Catholic, Unitarian Universalist, Jewish, and Islamic traditions, with 38 different Protestant denominations represented. The study also surveyed 2,049 clergy and 442 adult youth workers.

The study used commercial lists of faith-based institutions and a random methodology to select congregations for an invitation to participate in the study. Overall, 24% of the congregations invited to participate chose to do so. The teen participants were in grades 9–12 and represented a broad range of economic levels, ethnic backgrounds, geographic locations, and home situations. All the participants completed written surveys. The study also used interviews and focus groups involving youth, clergy, youth workers, and parents.

This study is the first of its size in recent years to look exclusively at the sexual values and behaviors of teens involved in congregational life. In addition, the study releases some of the first data related to teenagers and oral sex. Among its key findings:

- Ninety-four percent of the teens said that their faith is very important or important to them. They are very involved in congregational life and place a high priority on congregational activities. Seventy-one percent of the teens participate in two or more religious activities each week, in addition to attending worship services. Virtually all the teens said they are involved in some religious activity in addition to worship attendance, while only 1% percent of teens said that their faith is not important at all.

- Teens involved in faith-based institutions show rates of sexual intercourse which are significantly below those shown in secular studies. While data from the U.S. Centers for Disease Control and Prevention show that, across the country, 60.5% of 12th graders have had sexual intercourse, the *Faith Matters* survey shows that only 31% of 12th graders who are highly involved in congregational life have had sexual intercourse. The study also discusses a subgroup who are especially involved and have deep personal faith, among whom the percentage of 12th graders who have had intercourse drops to 16.5%.

- The congregationally involved teens take sexual intercourse seriously, but they are not in full agreement with their faith-based institutions concerning the morality of premarital intercourse. Ninety-three percent of teens agreed with this statement: "Sexual intercourse should only happen between people who have a commitment to each other." The same percentage believe their congregation thinks that premarital intercourse is wrong, but only 54.1% of the teens personally agree that it is wrong. One-third of the teens in the study are absolutely committed to waiting until they are married before having intercourse, but two-thirds of these young people think that they might have sex before marriage, and by the senior year, eight in ten think they might.

- While many religious teens are not having sexual intercourse, they are involved in other sexual behaviors, including oral sex. Twenty-nine percent of the 11th and 12th grade males and 26% of the 11th and 12th grade females say they have had oral sex. Alarmingly, the majority of teens surveyed (55%) think that they cannot contract a sexually transmitted disease from oral sex. The study also found that among 11th and 12th grade congregationally involved teens:

  — Seventy percent have fondled a partner's breasts and/or genitals.

  — Half have been nude with a member of the opposite sex.

- Eighty-nine percent of males and 71% of females masturbate.
- Almost all have kissed a member of the opposite sex.

- Youth from congregations which provided young people with information about contraception and sexually transmitted disease (about 8% of responding congregations) reported no instances of pregnancy or sexually transmitted disease. Youth from those congregations were not any more likely or less likely than other youth in the study to have had sexual intercourse.

- Youth from congregations that did not supply information on contraception and sexually transmitted disease were not so fortunate. Eleven percent of the females who have had intercourse have experienced a pregnancy. Nine percent of the youth who have had intercourse or oral sex reported having had a sexually transmitted disease.

- Half of the female teens who became pregnant chose to end that pregnancy with abortion. This included teens from denominational traditions which are strongly pro-life. In many instances, teens said that the potential disapproval of their families and congregations if they became unwed mothers played a role in the decision to have an abortion.

- Although 19% of teens said they have taken a pledge to remain a virgin until marriage, that subgroup was not any more or less likely than others in the study to have had sexual intercourse or to have experienced a pregnancy. That finding differs from a secular study that showed virginity pledges do delay premarital intercourse. It appears that the formal pledge does not have the same impact on teens who are already very involved in congregational life as it does on more secular teens.

- Sixty-two percent of the clergy who participated in the survey feel that faith-based institutions should teach teenagers both comprehensive sexuality education and abstinence. They favor trusting teenagers with full information about sexuality including what the Scriptures say and information on contraception and disease prevention. Thirty percent of the clergy preferred an abstinence-only approach to sexuality education, 4% felt that sexuality education should only be in the home, and 4% favored comprehensive sexuality education without an abstinence emphasis.

- Involvement in a faith-based institution does not protect teens against unwanted sexual experiences. Thirty-one percent of the 11th and 12th grade females surveyed said they have had such an experience. While force played a role, particularly in those instances where the unwanted experience was intercourse, social and emotional pressure and poor communication were greater factors. Ninety percent of the female teenagers would like programs from their faith-based institutions that would help them develop healthy assertiveness and avoid rape, sexual harassment, and sexual abuse.

- The study revealed a much higher percentage of congregationally involved teens who have a non-heterosexual orientation than clergy who participated in the study anticipated. Fourteen percent of the males and 11% of the females have a homosexual orientation, a bisexual orientation, or are uncertain of their orientation. Older teens have less uncertainty than younger teens. Most of the teens who feel they have a non-heterosexual orientation are not open about that with their clergy or their youth groups.

- Sixty-eight percent of the clergy agreed with this statement: "I think it is possible for us [as a congregation] to do more than we currently are in sexuality education, and I would like to make that a greater priority than it currently is." Another 24% of the clergy agreed that more should be done but felt unable to make it a priority at the present time.

- The teen participants in the *Faith Matters* survey gave their congregations poor grades in providing them with information about sexuality and with guidance to prepare for marriage and parenting. Clergy and adult youth workers, in contrast, gave themselves grades of fair or good for their work in those areas. Thus adult leaders in congregations see themselves doing a better job at providing information and guidance than their youth think they are doing. Teens were virtually unanimous in wanting their faith-based institutions to do more to help them relate their faith to dating, sexual decision-making, marriage, and parenting. They are very open to more help from their congregations, and they are frustrated with the overall failure of adult society to give them the help that they need.

Christian Community, Inc. is a nonprofit organization focused on research and program development to benefit congregations and the communities they serve. Past projects of the organization include work on church growth, congregational hospitality, congregational outreach to the poor, and stewardship. The organization is located in Fort Wayne, Indiana.

Faith Matters ISBN: 1-893270-10-6. For orders, please call 800–774–3360.